How to avoid CPS

A quick guide

By Leah Rusk

Table of Content

Chapter 1

What is CPS

Child Protective services. Child Welfare Services. Child Services. Department of Child and Protective Services. Department of Health and Human Services. Department of Child Services. Department of Child Safety. Department of Child and Family Services. Department of Children and Families. Many names for one agency with one goal.

Their main goal is to enforce child abuse laws and keep children safe. This can take many different forms. They investigation allegations of child abuse, provide referrals for services, create safety plans, allow parents to voluntarily place children outside the home while solving problems, and as a last resort, remove children from their home and place them in alternate homes or placements.

Surprisingly, CPS got its started from the Humane Society. Back in the 1800's, there were laws in place regarding animal abuse but none really that covered child abuse specifically. So the Humane Society founded an organization to start to advocate for child abuse laws and to investigate child abuse. The laws that you are more familiar with did not come into being until the 1970's when the federal government enacted the Child Abuse Prevention and Treatment Act. From that law sprang the different but similar state laws and regulations.

Children are considered a vulnerable population, along with the elderly and the mentally handicapped. They are smaller than most adults and they lack a lot of knowledge and experience that most adults have. They need to be protected until they are older and able to protect themselves. CPS is the arm of the government whose job it is to make sure that this vulnerable population is safe from abuse and neglect.

CPS is a government agency. It may be state or city or county run. Every state runs their CPS different. Even between counties, the CPS agencies may be run differently. Some states have started to outsource some aspects of CPS. If that is the case, they are under a contract with the local government and have all the powers and responsibilities of a government agent.

CPS operates under state child abuse laws. These laws differ wildly between states. This book will not be breaking down laws by state. Most states do have similar laws and views regarding child abuse though. Some enforcement may vary by county or city also. A rural location is going to have a different perspective on child rearing than a large urban city.

CPS enforces laws through court. What court enforces child abuse laws varies by state. Some states use juvenile court, some family court. No matter what court it is in, general court rules still apply. Dress appropriately. No inappropriate sayings or objects on your clothing. No hats or sunglasses (that are not required medically). Don't chew gum in the court room. Turn your phone off. Don't talk out of turn. Be early and be ready. All those things learned in school apply to the court room pretty well.

Chapter 2

Types of abuse

There are, at the end of the day, two types of child abuse. Neglect and abuse. Neglect means that the child is lacking basic needs. Abuse means physical harm to the child. Abuse can also be a threat of physical harm. Someone can be guilt of either abuse or neglect through their actions or their inactions. What that means is, if a parent or guardian allows someone to hit or hurt their child and takes no protective actions, it is abuse. Their inaction is the same as the abusive action that caused the injury. If a child is without food, a parent cannot blame the other parent for not buying it. The inaction of both parents to provide appropriate food for the child means they are both guilty of negligence. Let's break down each area and what CPS is looking for.

Neglect

In the eyes of the government, parents or guardians are required to provide the minimum sufficient level of care. But what does that mean? It means that the government understands that every parent and every family is different. Every child does not need a new bike every year or steak dinners every Friday. They do need a sufficient amount of food and appropriate clothing. Neglect can come in many forms in many places. Next we will look at different forms of neglect that CPS looks for.

Every human needs food. We all understand that. Children need food starting from day 1. What food they need changes a lot in the first few years. Parents are expected to understand what food a child needs and provide the appropriate amount. Appropriate nutrition is vital to a child's growth and development. A house should have safe and appropriate food in the home at all times.

A child deserves to live in a clean and safe home. No feces (human or animal) should be accessible to a child. Specifically young children who tend to put everything in their mouth. That also means that small objects like coins or batteries or uncooked pasta should not be on the floor where small children could eat it. Any home with toddlers or infants should always keep the floor clean and free of hazards at all times.

Children do not always see safety issues the same as adults. A broken wall outlet may look fun to play with to a child but is certainly unsafe. Broken boards with nails sticking out, broken windows, knives or scissors on or near the floor. Those are all safety hazards that CPS would take issues with.

Another safety issue that could occur in a home is unsafe people. Having people living in the home with a history of abusing children, violent acts, or recent drug use may be considered unsafe. Allowing unsafe people to babysit could also be considered negligent. Dealing drugs or prostitution out of a home means a lot of unknown and potentially unsafe people are in and out of the house often. This is a serious safety issue for children of any age. A parent is responsible in regards to who they allow in their home around their children.

Living in an RV, a tiny home, or on a boat is legal. Living in a car is not, by itself, illegal or child abuse. It could be though, if it is not safe or healthy for the child due to other circumstances. Medical conditions or freezing weather may be factors that make living in a car unsafe and negligent.

Children need regular medical visits and treatment for injuries. Not seeking medical treatment when necessary is neglect. If a child has a serious injury or illness, appropriate medical treatment is required. That could be a primary doctor, urgent care, or emergency care. Whatever treatment is needed, it should be done in a timely manner.

Medical advice also needs to be followed after a child is seen by a medical professional. Doctors are mandated reporters and will report if parents do not follow medical advice that could cause harm to a child. This could include not following up after major surgeries, not providing needed medical aids like special shoes or braces. A doctor may also be concerned if a child is not getting their prescribed medication as recommended. Again, this would be for something that could cause lasting or immediate damage.

Young children must be supervised at all time. As children get older their level of required supervision does change. Many states have laws regarding when a child is legally able to be home alone. Many states do not. See appendix A for state laws at time of publication. Either way, if a child is mentally unable to stay home alone safely then they still require supervision even if the law says they are old enough.

Siblings that are old enough to babysit can really help out around the home. A parent is required to assess their individual child's ability to babysit their siblings. If a child is required to do the majority of the parenting for their younger siblings it could lead to child neglect charges with CPS. A child required to parent their sibling's full time is not able to grow and be a normal child. They are also often under a lot of stress that can cause physical and mental health problems.

Some children are masters at escaping from their parent's supervision. If a child gets out of the home unnoticed and is found by other parties or law enforcement, the family is likely to get an investigation to see what is causing the lack of supervision. As children get older they will require less eyes on supervision. With all things, this varies by child. Children with mental or physical disabilities might need eyes on supervision longer than other children.

Abuse

Child abuse is a much more straight forward type of abuse. Generally, physical abuse leaves physical evidence. Children who are being physically abused may also have behavioral issues that are indicators that something is happening in the child's home life. Next we will briefly cover different types of abuse.

Physical

Physical discipline is legal in all states in the USA. Spanking with a hand is the common and most acceptable form of physical discipline. Once any injury is left on the child, it has gone beyond discipline and is now abuse. Any injury, no matter how small, can rise to that level. A bruise, a welt, a cut, or a broken bone could all lead to a finding of child abuse.

Assaulting a child at any time is illegal. Even if no injuries are left, it is still illegal. This includes throwing things at a child in anger, as well as physically hitting or harming. It is never appropriate to strike a child in anger, no matter what the child's actions are.

Babies cry and have no ability to tell you what they need. It can be frustrating at times for parents. Frustrated parents can make poor decisions and shake their baby to try to get them to listen or just to stop crying. This can cause severe brain injuries in infants. Their necks are not strong and any shaking can cause their brain to move and become injured. When this happens the child will likely be diagnosed with Shaken Baby Syndrome. Shaken Baby Syndrome can cause long term brain damage in children.

Sexual

Sexual abuse of children is any sexual touching of a child by a parent or caretaker. It is unnecessary to go into detail but do know that allowing a child around someone with a known history of sexually abusing children is illegal. It places the child at a very high risk of being abused. It is a parent's job to make every effort to protect their child from abuse.

Chapter 3

How to avoid involvement with CPS

So, now that we have explored all the reasons CPS might remove a child, what can a parent do to make sure the CPS does not have cause to be involved in their lives? Parenting is hard. Every day it is a struggle to take care of yourself and another living being (or multiple other living beings). Every day is filled with having to make decisions that affect everyone then second guessing those decisions.

Just to have it said, even if a parent does literally everything rights, CPS can still end up investigating. Anyone can call CPS to report suspected abuse or neglect. They don't have to have proof or know for sure that something has or will happen. They are only required to have a sincere belief or concern and not be intentionally lying. The majority of investigations done by CPS do not go anywhere. They are closed within a few weeks with no action taken by CPS other than possibly providing resources to help with general needs.

Although filing false reports is illegal, it is very difficult for law enforcement to prosecute people for that in regards to CPS reports. First, they don't want to discourage people from reporting. People should not have to be concerned that they could face legal problems just because they have concerns for a child. Second, people can report anonymously. Tracking down someone that reports anonymously is very time consuming. And lastly, proving someone maliciously lied is very hard. In order to report, you don't need proof, so being wrong is ok. Proving someone reported maliciously, to the extent needed for court, is very difficult.

Although it is hard, it does happen that people can face legal consequences for malicious reporting. It takes a lot though. If someone reports multiple times and all the reports are blatantly false, then it can be something that is investigated and actions taken. Most times, if reports come in constantly from someone in regards to a family and are always false, CPS will often stop going out and investigating those allegations.

So let's look at some ways to avoid dealing with CPS.

Neglect

Food. This may seem like an easy one, but it is not for everyone. The expectation is that there is adequate and appropriate food in the home at all times. That doesn't mean that there can only be name brand healthy food. If the fridge is full of chicken nuggets and PBJ fixings, that's fine. It just has to be food that is clean and edible.

If you have an infant, having appropriate food for that child's age is important. Formula for infants. Baby food or soft foods and milk for toddlers. An unsure parent should ask their child's pediatrician. If a child is statistically underweight parents want to work closely with their pediatrician regarding diet. There are also occupational therapists that can help children of all ages with problems eating.

Safe and appropriate housing is necessary for kids. Housing needs to be safe in that nothing is going to fall and injure a child, nothing is broken causing sharp edges, or exposed electrical wiring. Parents should be constantly making sure a home is safe. If an area cannot be made safe it should be secured so that children do not have access. In general, electricity, water, heating, and cooling are needed for homes. Some things are not necessary in all locations. If you don't live in an area that has inclement weather, heating or cooling may not be necessary. If you are not able to have running water for whatever reason, access to water and showers is necessary. If needed, going to the gym regularly for showers is appropriate. Also, using bottled water for drinking, cleaning, and basic washing is also acceptable. Working toilets are necessary. Again, if there is water in order to flush and keep them functional then they would be considered working. Electricity is generally always required but in some rural areas it may not be a standard for the community.

Housing can be a very difficult for families at times. Some parents don't have as much control over the condition of the house. A family may live with someone who continually makes the home unsafe. If that is the case, the best way to deal with it is to close off sections of the home that the children can play and be active in. Other parts of the home that are not safe, the children cannot go to or be in without strict supervision. Also, if the home is a rental and the landlords are not willing or able to maintain the property safely, then the parents may not be able to keep the home fully safe. In that situation, the parents can either control where the children can go or they may be forced to find other living arrangements. Another option is to call a local (city or county) housing authority to help with getting the home repaired and safe.

If a child likes to try to get out of the home and run around the neighborhood, extra measures will need to be taken. Window and door alarms can help to alert a parent when an escape is being attempted, as well as when someone enters the home. Extra locks on outside gates can also help. There are child safe door knob covers that keep doors from being opened. Without medical need, parents cannot put outside locks on a child's bedroom door. It is a safety hazard if there is a fire or other emergency. There are some medical conditions that require secure sleeping situations but that must be discussed with a doctor or other medical professional beforehand. It would be a good idea to have documentation of that need for secure sleeping on hand, at home, just in case anyone has concerns.

All medication needs to be kept secure. Medication needs to be placed out of reach of small children. This includes children's vitamins. They can be tasty and young children can overdose on them. If there are prescribed narcotics in the home they should be kept locked up or in a place that is inaccessible to children. If there teenagers in the home with known addiction issues, all medication should be securely locked up. If a parent or other household member uses needles or other types of medical sharps, a medical sharps container should always be used to dispose of them.

As laws are changing, marijuana is becoming legal in many states. Parents can legally use marijuana the same as everyone else. But, like alcohol, they must use it responsibly. Driving while high with a child in the car is obviously illegal. Being the primary caretaker of young children while high is also going to be a CPS concern. A young child needs a clear headed capable caretaker at all times. If there is an emergency, an adult needs to be able to figure out what needs to happen and do it. That action could be calling 911, driving a child to an ER, or just assessing an injury. So, at all times, a clear headed adult needs to be present to make vital emergency decisions. The parent is responsible to know when they may not be capable of caring for their children. This may be due to medication, alcohol or drug consumption, or post-surgery. Having a plan in place for someone to care for the child is vital.

Marijuana also causes problems with storage. Marijuana comes in a lot of forms now, and with that comes edibles. Edibles are just as legal as other marijuana, in legal states, but it must be stored safely. A lot of edibles are sugary treats which attract small children. It is not recommended to keep them in locations that children can access. That applies to any age child. If there are edibles in the home they should be locked away. The best and safest way is to have a separate fridge with a lock, generally kept in the garage. The same for non-refrigerated marijuana products. Keep them in a locked safe or container in a room that children do not have access to. Also remember that marijuana is oily. If marijuana is being processed or rolled, it should be on a surface that can be cleaned and not a surface that is touched by children. Something like a cutting board or cloth that can be immediately cleaned and put away is best.

To ER or not to ER

Children get sick and hurt. It is in their nature. Parents have to constantly assess injuries and determine the best course of action, without a medical degree. It is not always an easy job. If parents are able, they should read up on basic first aid or take a first aid course if they don't feel they have the knowledge needed to make these assessments. It is also important to have basic medical supplies. Band-aids of multiple sizes, antibiotic cream, ice packs, and alcohol wipes or similar; those make a good basic first aid kit for day to day injuries.

Some injuries are going to be more extensive than a layperson can handle. It is not always easy to know when to go to the emergency room (or urgent care if available in your area). It is easy to know that a child will need to go to emergency room (ER) for a broken bone or large cut/laceration. Children also need to see a doctor quickly if they hit their head hard on a solid surface.

Some injuries are less obvious. Injuries on the feet and hands are not always easy to detect in children. First, a lot of children don't want to stop playing so they will ignore pain in hands and feet in order to keep running around. Second, there are a lot of small bones and tendons in hands and feet. When they are injured, it is not always obvious how extensive they are injured. It may not show up as a serious injury for hours or days. Parents should keep an eye on hand and feet injuries for a few days to make sure they were not worsening.

Supervision

Children's supervision levels change over time. As they get older, parents want them to have more freedoms to be able to learn independently and grow more responsible. They don't need constant eyes on supervision as they grow older. They can play in their room by themselves when they are older. They can play outside as they get older. When these changes happen will vary by child. Some children, due to mental or physical disabilities, may not be able to be home alone until they are near adulthood if ever.

Some children need more supervision and safety measures than others. There are children that just love to escape and be free, with or without clothing. Those children will need more supervision and safety measures in order to keep them safe. More locks or alarms on doors and windows. More eyes on supervision. In home security cameras may also assist for times when a parent cannot be in the same room as a child. Remember, cameras cannot go into bathrooms or teenagers bedrooms. Children do have a level of privacy they are allowed as well as videos in bathrooms can rise to the level of being illegal.

Abuse

The line between discipline and abuse can be confusing to some but it is fairly black and white. Any discipline that leaves physical marks or injuries is considered abuse. Bruises, abrasions, lacerations, and even red marks that are still present when CPS arrives will be considered abuse. If your child bruises easily, it will still be considered abuse even if it is an average spanking.

The easiest way to avoid this concern is to not use physical discipline. There are a lot of other discipline techniques that work. I won't go into them here as there are plenty of books that cover them in depth. A counselor or therapist can also help to come up with a good structured discipline plan.

Grabbing a child in order to keep them from being injured is not abuse, even if injuries are left. Grabbing a child by the arm to stop them from running into the street, or pushing a hand away from a hot surface are all acceptable situations that injuries can occur.

There is never a reason to hit or strike or push a child in anger. Aside from being considered abuse by CPS, it is also possibly criminally considered assault. That isn't to say that parenting isn't frustrating or that parents don't get angry. Physical violence is not the answer. When a parent gets angry the best option is the put the child in a safe location (room or crib) and step away to calm down. Go scream into a pillow or call a supportive friend in order to get the frustrations out. Then go back to parenting safely.

Babies are particularly vulnerable to physical abuse. They can cry and parents have no idea why or how to help them. Frustration can come out in the form of yelling and sometimes shaking an infant. Shaking a baby can cause their brains to hit the side of their skull, causing trauma and possibly long term damage. Frustrated parents should place their infant in a safe place and walk away to calm down. Calling a supportive family member can help also. Yelling at or around an infant has been shown to cause harm. Infants and young children have not gained the ability to regulate their adrenaline. If there is constant turmoil, violence, anger, or yelling in the home, infants and toddlers can have higher adrenaline levels that they are unable to regulate or bring back down. This can cause long term problems with self-regulation. If arguments are going to occur between parents, it should be done away from a child in a safe manner with minimal yelling. If that doesn't appear to be possible, have the child out of the house with family or babysitters to have time to deal with stressful issues.

Chapter 4

What to do if CPS knocks: questions and answers

Do I have to talk to CPS if they knock on my door?

No. With CPS you have the same rights as you do with any other law enforcement type agency. You do not have to talk to them. You do not have to allow them into your home. You do not have to allow them access to your child(ren). CPS does always have the option to go to court and file for either (depending on location) court orders to investigate or court orders to bring the child(ren) into custody. If they are given orders to investigate it may include multiple different things. They may be able to enter the home with or without permission. They may be able to interview the children. They may also be able to get a court order to require the parents (or guardians) to take a drug test. It will all depend on what the allegations are. If the allegations are severe enough the court may order the children brought into custody immediately in order to make sure they are safe.

If CPS does knock on your door and you are unsure of how things may turn out, you should politely tell them that you will be hiring at attorney who will get in touch with them as soon as possible. Then contact a family law attorney with CPS experience at the next available moment. Do whatever they tell you to do. They will likely recommend talking to CPS with them present.

Can they talk to my child at school?

In all states, to the best of my knowledge, CPS is allowed to go into a school and interview a child without parental permission. Some states do have rules regarding this so it does vary a lot between locations. In some locations you can tell the worker or agency not to go to the school without permission in the future. Not all jurisdictions are required to follow this request.

If you are concerned about CPS talking to your child at school or it is a constant problem (due to family or custody disputes), you are welcome to tell your child that they should not talk to CPS without you present. CPS cannot force a child to talk and children are welcome to leave at any time. If your child is old enough and there is cause, let them know they are never required to talk to anyone without you present. This is helpful in regards to many possible situations, like talking to police or school employees that may cause more problems than good. It is always important to make the distinction between talking to law enforcement (or school personal) when you need help and talking to them when they are accused of doing something wrong.

Can they come into my house?

You have the right not to allow anyone into your home that you do not want there. They cannot enter without permission from someone in the home or a court order. A worker should ask for permission to enter every single time they visit your home.

When do I get an attorney?

This is a hard question to answer. In general, you should get an attorney any time you are concerned for yourself or your child. Do know that most CPS investigations do not lead to anything happening. A lot of calls come in that are due to custody disputes and are lies or exaggerations. Some calls come in due to family disputes. If grandparents are not allowed to visit the grand children or there is a dispute over estates, allegations can be made out of anger or retaliation. Schools sometimes make reports over concerns that are not how they look after investigating. Children can make fantastical tales to explain injuries or accidents.

In order to determine if you should hire an attorney, ask the worker what the allegations are that they are investigating. If they are obviously and provable false then an attorney may not be needed. If they are serious and grounded in some level of truth, it may be a good idea to hire an attorney to protect yourself and the children. If you are in the middle of a contentious divorce or custody battle, then you should involve an attorney.

<u>Bonus : What is a mandated reporter?</u>

A mandated reporter is someone who, based on their profession, is legally required to report any concerns of child abuse or neglect. This legal requirement is generally directly linked to any license required for them to do their job. They do not have to have proof of child abuse. They do not have to have all the information about any incident. They only have to suspect that something might have happened or be happening. If they fail to report, they can incur sanctions with their license, loss of license, and although rare, criminal charges.

Mandated reports exist in all states. All medical personnel (doctors, nurses) are mandated reporters. All educational staff are mandated reporters. Therapist and counselors are also mandated reporters. CPS workers are also mandated reporters. In some locations, some utility workers are also mandated reporters. That one does seem weird but they are in homes all the time and see children often.

Chapter 5

Resources

If you are struggling there are resources out there to help you before it gets to the point of CPS involvement.

211

211 is the nationwide number to research local social services. You can also find 211 on the internet at 211.org. This service can give you a list of local resource to help in many different areas.

Library

Libraries have more services then most people know. There are infant, toddler, and small child reading or activity groups. These can give you a little bit of a break and vent to parents in the same situations you are in. They also have parenting books and videos. Reading a parenting book can provide ideas on how to handle your child's specific behaviors. It is unlikely everything in the book will work but most have at least one or two things that should help most families.

Fire station

Fire stations are a safe surrender location. If you have a newborn (age varies by state) this is a place you can drop your child off if you feel you cannot care for the child. You can do this anonymously if you choose. Fire stations can also help you with car seat installation and information.

Churches

Churches are an amazing resource in many communities. Many have resources or connections that can help with an

array of needs and they do not often require you to be a
member of their church to access these resources. Larger
churches often have counseling services, drug rehab
groups, and used clothing or furniture resources. Smaller
churches may offer these services also. Churches are often
involved in food bank resources as well. Many churches
offer daycare services and may have scholarships or
income based assistance available. They may have
parenting groups that meet in their building also, to give
you a wider support system.

Chapter 6

Conclusion

Having children is one of the best times and most trying, stressful times in your life. Parents go through a lot in their 18+ years. It is not always easy or fun. Making the best choices every day for a child is an important task and lofty goal. The best thing any parent can do is try hard and ask for help when they needed it. A family with a solid support system does much better then someone without help. Everyone needs support and help sometimes.

Appendix A

Minimum age to be home alone by state as of publication date.

State	Minimum Age
Nevada	No specified age
New Hampshire	No specified age
New Jersey	No specified age
New Mexico	10
New York	No specified age
North Carolina	8
North Dakota	9
Ohio	No specified age
Oklahoma	No specified age

Oregon	10
Pennsylvania	No specified age
Rhode Island	Unknown
South Carolina	No specified age
South Dakota	No specified age
Tennessee	10
Texas	No specified age
Utah	No specified age
Vermont	Unknown
Virginia	No specified age
Washington	10
West Virginia	Unknown
Wisconsin	No specified age

Wyoming	Unknown